AN AMERICAN PIONEER

Macdonald

Contents

Introduction   5

Westport Landing   6

Storm on the Prairie   8

Stampede   10

Nooning   12

The Campfire   14

The Sioux Encampment   16

Fort Laramie   19

Independence Rock   20

Snake River Valley   22

In the Mountains   25

Safe at Last   26

Picture Glossary   28

Finding Out More   30

Introduction

This book tells the story of Beth and Hannah, two sisters who set off in 1845 with their parents to make the long trek westwards across America along the Oregon trail. Their journey from Maryland to Oregon was over 2100 miles long and took six months. It was hard going; many of their companions fell sick; some died and were buried alongside the trail.

Beth and Hannah were travelling to join their uncle. He had left the Eastern States of America two years previously with a group of missionaries, and was now preaching and teaching among the Nez Perce Indians, who lived in Oregon. His letters described Oregon as a beautiful but harsh land, with high mountains, steep valleys, great forests and rushing mountain streams. The winters were long and cold, but the brief summers were warm enough to grow good crops of corn and vegetables. He was happy there. Beth and Hannah's parents decided to make the dangerous journey to join him.

The missionaries were not the first people to travel westwards across America. For many years, fur trappers and traders had journeyed there. They had established a few permanent settlements, called forts. These forts were like small towns with shops, and workshops for blacksmiths and carpenters. Soon, Indians came to the forts to trade. Many traders married Indian women, and settled down peacefully to live near the forts.

Beth and Hannah and their family were among the earliest migrants to travel westwards. In the years that followed, many more people settled in the lands along the Oregon trail. Tragically, they often treated the Indians very badly, and drove them from their homelands.

Some of the objects used by the pioneers are illustrated at the end of this book. There are also pictures of the wildlife that lived along the Oregon trail. In addition there are suggestions for places to visit and books to read.

Westport Landing

'This is where our real journey starts,' said Pa, gazing out over the wide prairie. Beth and Hannah Richardson stared at their father in astonishment, hardly able to believe their ears. They had travelled such a long way already! About three weeks ago, they had left their old home in Massachusetts, on the east coast of America. Now they had arrived at the busy town of Westport, on the Missouri river, after many days in a bumpy stagecoach, and a long and cramped voyage in a crowded steamboat.

'Yes, girls,' said their father, excitedly. 'This is the start of the wagon trail to Oregon!'

Beth and Hannah's uncle was a missionary in Oregon, a beautiful land in the far west of America, across the Rocky Mountains. He had asked Pa to come and help him with his preaching to the Indians. 'Bring Martha and the girls, as well,' he had written in his letter. 'There's plenty of land and food, and a good life for everyone here.'

At Westport, the Richardsons found many other families camped near the landing place. They were

waiting until enough people had arrived to make up a wagon train. It was not safe to travel in small groups, for fear of attack by Indians.

When about twenty families were ready and waiting, Mr Richardson called a meeting.

'We must hire a guide to show us the way,' he said. 'What about Joel Carter?'

Beth and Hannah were rather frightened of Joel. He was very tall, with a bushy black beard and a huge, roaring voice.

'But don't worry, he's not as wild as he looks,' said Beth. 'Pa chose him because he knows the mountains well. He used to be a fur trapper. We'll need him to show us the way. There aren't any roads or signposts where we're going.'

Pa and Joel and the other families agreed on a day when they would start on the long trek. One by one, they got their lumbering ox wagons into line. Joel blew a long blast on his bugle and they set off, across the vast, empty prairie. Pa led the way, with Beth by his side. Ned, their dog, skipped after them.

'This is better than being cramped up on that boat!' he seemed to say.

Storm on the Prairie

It was daybreak. The camp guards fired their rifles to waken everybody. Beth and Hannah stumbled sleepily out of their tent.

'Let's hope there's something different to look at today,' grumbled Hannah. 'I just can't face any more grass!'

But the grassy prairie stretched away into the distance as far as they could see. They had been

travelling along the Oregon trail for over a fortnight now. It was boring and uncomfortable sitting in the wagon day after day, with nothing to watch but the shadows of clouds moving over the grass. Sometimes Beth and Hannah walked, to lighten the load for the oxen, but after a while they grew tired, and climbed up into the wagon again.

Pa came back from helping to lead the horses out to graze. Ma was making coffee and toasted cornmeal cakes for breakfast.

'My, that smells good!' Pa said. 'I'm as hungry as a horse this morning!'

'Pa, why don't you let the horses and mules roam free at night to graze, like the oxen?' asked Beth.

'Because this is Indian country,' replied Pa. 'The Indians don't think it's wrong to steal horses, and so they might come to our camp in the night and take them away. But the Indians won't take our oxen because they don't need them.'

By six o'clock the wagons were ready to set off. Beth and Hannah went to look for their friend, Jesse Appleyard. His family were farmers, and Jesse liked to boast of how much he knew about raising animals and growing crops.

'Your pa's only a preacher,' he said. 'He won't know how to make a living out West. I bet I could teach him a thing or two!'

Suddenly Pa Richardson shouted, 'Big clouds coming up, everybody, black as the back of a frying pan! Take cover! Quick, Martha, get the girls into the wagon and check that everything's tied down!'

The huge, threatening clouds piled up and blotted out the sunlight. A blinding flash lit up the sky over their heads. The wind whipped at the canvas wagon cover and snatched it out of Ma's hand. Beth and Hannah clung to her as sheets of stinging rain drove into the wagon. When the canvas was at last lashed down, they huddled together on top of the wet blankets and furniture.

'Can't we stop and shelter somewhere?' gasped Hannah.

'There is no shelter,' said Ma, giving the girls a squeeze. 'And we have to keep going, or we won't get across the mountains before the snows come.'

Stampede

'Ouch!' cried Hannah, rubbing the side of her head.

Ma looked up from her knitting. 'What's the matter, child?' she asked.

Beth had seen what happened. 'Hannah banged her head against that wooden box when the wagon jolted,' she explained to Ma. 'She's such a cry-baby!'

'Don't be mean, Beth,' said Ma. 'You know Hannah isn't well.'

Secretly, Ma was worried. Hannah had been lying ill in a makeshift bed in the wagon for several days. She had the sickness the trekkers called Camp Fever. Other families had it too. Ma thought that perhaps Hannah had caught it from drinking muddy river water, and she knew that people sometimes died from it, too.

The wagon lurched on. The trekkers were following the River Platte westwards to the mountains. The

trail was hard going, with great ruts and cracks across it.

'We'll be lucky not to break a wheel-axle going over one of those!' Pa said.

While Hannah was ill, Beth spent more time talking to Joel, their guide. He showed her the tracks made by coyotes and wolves, and explained that the ruts across the tracks were made by buffalo.

'At this time of year, the pools on the high plains dry up, and so the buffalo come down to the river to drink, thousands and thousands of them!'

A sudden shout made them both turn round. Jesse Appleyard came rushing up to Joel. 'Buffalo! There's buffalo coming!' he yelled.

Joel looked up sharply towards the hills. There was a sound like distant thunder as the herd came pouring down the slope. 'They're stampeding!' he yelled. 'Something's frightened them. Get those wagons out of the way fast!'

There were shrieks of fear from the families at the back of the wagon train. The men urged their oxen into a lumbering gallop, until they too seemed to be stampeding. Joel flung Jesse and Beth into his wagon. Jesse bounced up and down with excitement.

'Look! I can see Indians!' he shouted. 'They're following the buffalo! How can they ride so well bareback? I'd fall off if I went that fast!'

'They're Pawnee Indians,' shouted Joel, smiling. 'And they can hunt just as well as they ride!'

Nooning

At midday the trekkers usually stopped for a rest and a meal – 'nooning time' they called it. As the days grew hotter, breakfast and nooning time seemed to grow further and further apart.

'Isn't it time to stop yet?' sighed Beth. Ned, the dog, followed faithfully beside her. He didn't bound and jump any more. His paws were sore and his coat was covered with dust.

The wagon train had now reached a wide, treeless plain, so dry and sunbaked that in many places nothing grew on it at all. To the left, they could see distant hills which had been blasted by the wind and sand into extraordinary shapes like church spires and chimney stacks. Each step the children took sent up a little puff of dust, and the wagon wheels raised great choking clouds. Only the people

riding in the first wagon of the train escaped the dust. Today, the Jackson family led the way, because Mrs Jackson was dangerously ill with Camp Fever.

Joel had gone ahead to find a good nooning place. 'There's a willow clump and a pool that's deep enough to wash in,' he reported. 'Let's stop there.'

'Water and shade, the Lord be praised!' cried Ma.

The line of wagons stopped beside the almost dried-up river. The willow clump was little more than a few scrubby bushes, no higher than Beth's head.

'No shade or firewood here,' said Ma, as brightly as she could, 'but there's water to wash your dresses, girls. Set out the food, Beth. And Hannah, you rest quietly. You mustn't tire yourself.'

Hannah sat by the wagon, watching Jesse collect dried buffalo dung for the campfire. There was nothing else to burn on the treeless plain. Jesse grinned, and threw a ball of dung at Hannah's head.

'Got you!' he shouted.

Hannah leaped up, and threw it back at him.

Ma came back from the river. 'Good Lord alive!' she exclaimed. 'What are those children doing?'

Pa only laughed. 'Hannah must be feeling better,' he said. 'Thank goodness.'

13

The Campfire

It was time to stop and set up camp for the night. They parked the wagons in a tight circle and chained them all together. In that way, the Indians couldn't take one away while they slept. Then each family pitched its tent, forming a ring round the wagons. They all lit campfires, too. Each family dug a trench in the ground, filled it with dry buffalo dung, and set fire to it. Soon the camp was guarded by a circle of glowing fires.

'We'll have pemmican pudding tonight,' called Ma. 'Get me the pemmican and the flour, Beth.'

Beth scrambled into the wagon and squeezed past Ma's spinning wheel and the butter churn to get to the big store chest at the back of the wagon. Carefully, she lifted down the clock that had belonged to Granny, and the big bacon sack that rested on top of the store chest. The sack felt heavy, but Beth knew that it was mostly full of bran, which shielded the bacon from the heat and stopped the fat melting and going bad. Inside the chest there were sealed boxes of coffee, and bags of rice, flour and beans. There was

also a small canvas bag. Beth tugged it out, then scooped some flour into a tin basin. She made sure that the lid of the chest was properly closed again and clambered back out of the wagon.

Ma opened the sack and poured out some coarse brown flakes. This was pemmican, made from dried and powdered buffalo meat. Joel had shown the trekkers how to prepare it. He had learned about it from the Indians. Now Ma boiled it over the campfire with flour to make a pudding. Beth and Hannah thought it tasted good. In the early days of the trek, Hannah had been so fussy that she wouldn't even eat her bacon rinds. Now she knew better!

After supper, Ma wrote in her diary and Pa read the Bible. Jesse's pa played his guitar, while Joel did a wild, stamping dance.

'That's the fandango,' he told them. 'I learned it from some Spaniards down in Santa Fe.'

The Sioux Encampment

'Fort Laramie in sight!' called Joel, who was riding at the head of the wagon train. Everyone gave a cheer.

'What a relief!' said Ma, smiling. 'We can do some proper washing at last! And, God willing, Jesse's mother will have her baby here.'

Hannah and Beth were still wearing the best dresses they had put on for poor Mrs Jackson's funeral. She had died of Camp Fever, and the trekkers had buried her by the side of the trail. Pa had read the prayers, and they had all sung hymns.

'Oh, my!' called Ma, from her seat high on the wagon. 'Do you see what I see? There's a great crowd of Indian tipis right in front of the fort.'

'The Indians won't harm us if we don't harm them,' said Pa. 'They're only waiting to trade with us.'

'Don't the Indians mind us coming into their land?' asked Beth.

'Yes, but there's lots of land; more than enough for everyone,' said Pa.

'Jesse's father says that the Indians don't deserve the land,' interrupted Hannah. 'He says they don't farm it, they just live off buffalo meat.'

'Hannah,' said Pa sternly, 'Don't ever let me hear you say such wicked things again!'

When the wagons reached the Sioux encampment Beth and Hannah begged to be allowed to meet the Indian children. Pa stopped the wagon beside a tipi where a group of women were scraping buffalo skins. One of them had three small girls with her. One girl held out the toy tipi she had been playing with.

'Does she want to give it to us?' asked Hannah.

'I think so,' replied Pa, 'but you must give her something in return.'

'We could give them one of our rag dolls,' suggested Beth. 'Would that do?'

'I should think so,' said Pa. 'Try and see.'

Beth found one of their dolls, and held it out to the Indian girl. She took it, and put the toy tipi into Beth's hands. She did not smile, but her eyes were warm and friendly.

Fort Laramie

'At least we shall sleep safely tonight,' said Ma, with a smile. 'It's good to see four walls and a roof again.'

The fort was a big, square whitewashed building, overlooking the River Platte. It had been built by the American Fur Company, and fur trappers, many of them Indians, came from hundreds of miles around to sell beaver and buffalo skins to the Company's buyers. With their earnings, the trappers bought guns and traps, and luxuries like coffee, sugar and tobacco at the fort's storehouse. For the trekkers, the fort was their last chance to buy food before they headed for the fearsome Rocky Mountains.

Beth and Hannah wandered round the big open space inside the fort. They saw groups of men waiting outside the carpenter's workshop while the carpenter mended broken wheels and patched up splintered wagons. They met Joel outside the smithy.

'Look at that wonderful horse over there,' he said. 'It's a Sioux mustang. The Indians breed them and bring them here to sell.'

He was interrupted by a loud bellowing.

'What's that?' cried Hannah, in alarm.

The smith had turned one of the oxen upside down, and it lay on its back in a trench, protesting loudly.

'Don't worry,' laughed Joel. 'He's only going to put new shoes on it! Oxen get sore feet as they plod along, and new shoes make them more comfortable. An ox won't stand still to be shod, and so the smith has to get at its feet like that.'

'Mind out!' called one of Joel's trapper friends, as a mule laden with huge bundles pushed its way through the crowd. He smiled at Hannah.

'Want to see some hairy banknotes?' he said, pointing to one of the bundles.

'Hairy banknotes! What are they?' asked Hannah and Beth together.

'He means furs,' explained Joel. 'They used to be called hairy banknotes because they were worth such a lot of money. But I reckon there's more money to be made as a guide nowadays. Now, youngsters, you run along back to your Ma and help her with that washing.'

Independence Rock

They had left Fort Laramie far behind. Now the wagons toiled up towards the Rocky Mountains. The path was covered with stones and boulders. It was hard work for the oxen; they were beginning to look thin and tired. Sometimes they had to stumble on all day without a drink because the streams were bitter and tasted of soda.

One afternoon, Pa pointed towards a long granite rock that stood out in the middle of the plain.

'That's Independence Rock,' he said. 'Today we'll break the rules and make our camp early.'

'Why is it called Independence Rock?' asked Beth.

'Joel Carter told me its name,' said Pa. 'He says that all wagon trains heading west aim to reach it by Independence Day. It's the sixth of July today, so we're only two days late. Do you want to climb the Rock with me and Ma before supper?'

They all set off towards the Rock.

'Wait for me!' shouted Jesse. 'I'm coming too! Pa said I had to keep clear of our wagon this afternoon, so I can come and climb the Rock with you. I'll race you to the top!'

The climb to the top was easier than it looked. When they got there, they were surprised to see lots of names carved into the surface of the Rock.

'They're the names of people who've travelled this way before us,' said Pa.

'Can we add our names too?' asked Beth.

Pa got out his knife and began to carve. He wrote 'Richardsons to Oregon, 6 July 1845'.

'Put Jesse's name, too,' said Beth. 'We can't leave him out.'

'I've carved mine already,' said Jesse, proudly.

'Then carve Ned's name,' said Beth. 'Please, Pa.'

'Ned's a Richardson, so he's included,' laughed Pa. 'We must climb down now and get on with the supper. It's rabbit pie, I think.'

Back at the wagons, Jesse's father was waiting for them with a big smile on his face.

'Jesse,' he called. 'Come and say hello to your new baby sister!'

Snake River Valley

The wagon train wound its way through cold, high mountain passes. At last it was time to begin the slow descent down the westward slopes of the Rocky Mountains. This was the start of a nightmare journey over a stony wilderness. A few families left the main wagon train and turned southwards to take the California trail. Jesse and his family went with them.

The remaining wagons continued westwards into the valley of the Snake River, which flowed fast and deep and treacherous.

'We've got to cross to the other bank,' said Joel. 'Three Island Crossing is the safest place to try.'

Beth and Hannah could see the crossing place ahead of them; the islands were like three stepping stones in the river. They could see the dangerous current swirling between them, too.

'We must chain all the wagons together,' said Joel, 'or they'll be swept away.'

The men fastened the chains, and Pa told Ma and the girls to get inside the wagon and sit tight.

Slowly, the wagon train lumbered across the river. The leading wagons were already safe on the far bank when, all of a sudden, one of the frightened animals slipped and lost its footing. Ma and the girls were flung off their seats, as their wagon broke free from the rest of the train and lurched over on its side. The water poured in. Ma flung the terrified girls up on to the storage chest as the river swirled through the wagon up to her waist.

'Quick! Get a rope!' shouted someone on the bank.

The girls clung to Ma in terror. They felt the wagon lurch and heard its wheels crunch on the river bed. Pa was on the bank now, with Joel and several other men, hauling the wagon towards dry land. Once the oxen felt firm ground under their feet they pulled bravely and hauled the wagon clear of the water.

That night at camp Ma checked through the stores of food in the wagon. They were nearly all ruined.

'We must be brave,' said Pa. 'We are all alive and unharmed. Let us thank the Lord for that!'

In the Mountains

At last the wagon train reached the first of the snowcapped mountains of Oregon. The trekkers were too tired to enjoy the beauty all around them. Joel led them down deep gorges, and across narrow ridges with steep precipices on either side. But they could only think of their poor oxen, now so wasted with hunger and exhaustion that they could hardly lift their feet. The trekkers knew that without oxen to pull their wagons they would all die in the mountains. They shuddered at the thought.

'We must make the wagon lighter, or these animals will fall to their knees,' said Pa. 'An ox won't fall until it's almost dead, but once it's down, the poor beast never gets up again.'

So they threw out the spinning wheel and the clock that had belonged to Granny, and the brass bedstead.

'You can throw out the store chest too,' said Ma. 'There's almost nothing left in it to eat.'

Beth and Hannah always felt hungry. They learned to look out for edible fungus and berries in the forest. They even chewed roots. One day, the wagon train passed an encampment of Nez Perce Indians.

'Look over there at all that washing hung out to dry,' said Hannah.

'That's not washing, it's pieces of salmon drying,' said Ma. 'Pa, can we trade something for it?'

'What have we got to bargain with?' asked Pa.

'For food, I'd trade the clothes off our backs!' exclaimed Ma. She tore off her shawl and apron, and took some faded dresses from the back of the wagon. Then she brought out her comb and mirror and the big copper kettle. It didn't look much, but perhaps it would buy a little to eat.

The Indians seemed kind and friendly, and showed by their looks that they were sorry for the weary travellers. They gave Ma a whole basket of dried salmon in return for the old clothes and the copper kettle. One of the women beckoned to Hannah.

'See!' she said, offering her a plant with strange fleshy roots. 'Eat! it's good! You grow well soon. I know missionaries; they helped my child, so now I help you!'

Safe at Last

A few weeks later, Beth and Hannah, Ma and Pa,
were sitting down with all their Oregon cousins to
enjoy the splendid welcome feast that Auntie Cary
had prepared for them. There was melon and salmon
and pumpkin pie. Friends and neighbours came to
join them. The trekkers felt exhausted but happy.

'How lucky we are to be here,' Beth thought. She
liked the pretty Willamitte Valley where Uncle Adam
lived and worked. It looked safe and snug. Her
uncle's log cabin had a little garden with a shed for
cows and a vegetable patch. He had cleared enough
forest to plant a field of oats and another of wheat.
Soon Pa would build a house and make a garden, too,
before he joined Uncle Adam in his work, preaching
and teaching at the Mission.

Some families had not been so lucky, Beth thought.
She remembered all the people who had begun the
long trail to Oregon but who had not reached their
journey's end. The last part of the trail had been the
worst. The trail had led them to the Columbia River,
which ran through a deep gorge with steeply wooded

cliffs on either side. There was no path below the cliffs, and so they had had to build makeshift rafts and sail down the river. It had been terrifying. The river was fast and icy cold. Once the wagons had been lashed to the rafts they were set adrift in the racing current. There was no way of steering them. Beth and Hannah would never forget the cries of a family whose raft had struck a sunken rock. It broke up immediately, and within seconds the wagon and its passengers had been swept away.

Looking at the happy faces around the long wooden table outside her uncle's log cabin, Beth felt that this meal was perhaps just a wonderful dream, and that she would soon wake up and find herself on board the terrifying raft again.

'Poor Beth is tired out,' said Auntie Cary, as she brought in a big dish of pancakes and put it on the table. 'I don't wonder, after all she's been through! Now, eat up, everybody, you're here at last, safe and sound in your new home!'

'Yes, safe at last!' said Pa. 'May God be thanked!'

Picture Glossary

The travellers who set off along the Oregon trail were journeying through lands which were largely uncharted and unknown to the people who lived in the eastern states of America. Few 'easterners' had ever left their own states, and few had ever met any of the Indian peoples whose ancestors had lived in America long before the settlers from Europe arrived, about 250 years before this story begins.

The travellers saw many new and interesting sights on their journey. They walked across vast, flat prairies, where dry grass stretched as far as the eye could see, past rocks sculpted into strange shapes by the relentless desert wind, and into steep, wooded valleys and deep gorges.

Many of the animals who lived in these lands were new and strange to the travellers. Some were majestic, like the eagles which soared high above the mountain passes. Others, like the rattlesnakes they met in the desert, were deadly poisonous. The long trail was an exciting, and sometimes dangerous, adventure.

Above: What the pioneers took with them
1 Double-barrelled shotgun.
2 Three-legged skillet for cooking over open fires.
3 Butter churn.

Right: The Oregon Trail
The journey to the 'New Land' was long and hard and took the pioneers over a vast area of America. Only sick people and very young children could ride in the wagons. The rest had to walk. There simply wasn't room for passengers in the packed wagons which carried all the pioneers' belongings. The pioneers passed through lands inhabited by various Indian tribes, and these are shown on the map.

4 Trunk covered with ox-hide.
5 Yoke for oxen.
6 Patchwork quilt.
7 Herbal medicines.
8 Clock.

SIOUX
INDIANS

Iowa

Missouri River

Independence
Rock

PAWNEE
INDIANS

Fort
Laramie

Platte River

OREGON TRAIL

Missouri

Westport
Landing

Kansas River

**Above: Animals seen along the
Oregon trail**
 9 Buffalo
10 Prairie dog
11 Eagle
12 Raccoon
13 Porcupine
14 Pronghorn (deer)
15 Coyote
16 Rattlesnake
17 Grizzly bear

Finding Out More

Books to Read

The following books contain information about the American West:

D. Brown **The Westerners** (Michael Joseph 1974)
B. Currie **Pioneers in the American West, 1780–1850** (Longman 1980)
H. Horn **The Pioneers** (Time-Life 1974)
R. May **The American West** (Macmillan 1982)
R. May **Our World Wallcharts: The American West** (Macmillan 1979)
R. Utley **Indian Soldier and Settler** (Washington University Press 1977)
D. Wise **The American West** (Macmillan 1984)

You may need an adult to help you read this book, but it contains a great deal of interesting information:
D. Lavender **Westward Vision: the Story of the Oregon Trail** (McGraw Hill 1985)

Places to Visit

The following museums have displays of American life in pioneer times:
Bath: The American Museum, Claverton Manor
Edinburgh: The Royal Scottish Museum
Glasgow: Glasgow Corporation Art Gallery and Museum
London: The Museum of Mankind

The John Judkyn Memorial, Freshford Manor, Bath, Avon, lends teaching packs, displays and tapes to schools. It has several items about the American West in its collections.

Kilverstone New World Wildlife Park, Thetford, Norfolk has collections of (living) animals from America, and can be visited.